Ma, can I be a feminist and still like men?

Ma, can I be a feminist and still like men?

Lyrics from life by Nicole Hollander

St. Martin's Press   New York, New York

Library of Congress Cataloging in Publication Data

Hollander, Nicole.
  "Ma, can I be a feminist and still like men?"

   1.   Feminism—Caricatures and cartoons.   2.   American
wit and humor, Pictorial.   I.   Title.
NC1429.H588A4   1980   741.5'973   79-26978
ISBN 0-312-03611-6 pbk.

The informational captions were contributed by Karen Wellisch.

Thank you Karen, Michael, Paul, Mom, Jana, Arlene, Suzy and Margo.
This book is dedicated to you, and to everyone who ever wanted to have the last word.

Some Introductory Remarks from Sylvia

Mystery & Romance

She slapped him—he caught her arm and pressed her to him in a grip of steel; she felt his long arrogant taut thighs in his long taut jeans burning into her flesh. Her breath grew shallow; her nipples hardened, like two tiny pebbles, like sweet hard candy, like two finishing nails.

Oh how she hated him—Yet her body flamed with desire for him.

.... *Wayward Nipple-s*

What was the secret
at Edgemere Castle?
Why was the darkly
attractive Lord Brindle
so taciturn, and
why was little Rudolph
so little?

IT RAINED THE AFTERNOON OF MOTHER'S FUNERAL. THAT MORNING I DISCOVERED THAT UNCLE GEOFFREY HAD EMBEZZLED THE FAMILY FORTUNE, LOSING HEAVILY ON THE GREYHOUNDS AND LEAVING ME PENNILESS AND POORLY EDUCATED. THERE WAS BARELY ENOUGH MONEY TO BURY MY DELICATE, ARISTOCRATIC MOTHER. HER BODY SO THIN, SO LIGHT, SO LIKE THE TINY WHIPPED CREAM FILLED MARZIPAN CAKES SHE DELIGHTED IN BEFORE THE SHADOW OF THAT DREAD REMORSELESS DISEASE CLAIMED HER . . . BUT I DIGRESS. THAT AFTERNOON I HAD BURIED THE PAST AND HAD NO INTIMATION OF WHAT LAY AHEAD AS I EAGERLY RIPPED OPEN A HEAVY CREAM COLORED ENVELOPE, FROM ITALY, EMBOSSED WITH A STRANGELY FAMILIAR BARONIAL CREST . . . A LETTER THAT WAS TO LEAD ME FAR FROM MY HOME AND STRAIGHT INTO THE . . .

Arms of Evil

when I was young, my mother used to say to me: "Remember Rita, Veronica Lake had better things to do than to hang around the phone waiting for Alan Ladd to call."

Unfortunately, around 1962
I fell under the influence
of Sandra Dee and threw
my life away.

AND NOW I'D LIKE TO SING A MEDLEY OF THE LYRICS THAT RUINED OUR LIVES. PLEASE HUM ALONG USING ANY CAROLE KING MELODY.

Oh BABY/ I WAS BARELY BREATHIN', I WAS JUST TREADING WATER 'TIL I MET YOU/ NOW THAT I HAVE YOU I DON'T NEED NO OTHER RAISON D'ÊTRE/ I DON'T EVEN NEED TO LEAVE THE HOUSE/ OH BABY WHEN WE'RE TOGETHER I'M MISERABLE and BORED/ BUT WHEN WE'RE APART THE SUN DON'T SHINE/

OH BABY COME BACK TO ME/ I NEED YOUR KINDA LOVING/ SINCE YOU'VE BEEN GONE I CAN'T EVEN TIE MY SHOES/ OFTEN I EAT Rice Krispies for dinner/ OH BABY...

THE MOTEL WAS A DIRTY PINK, CRAMPED AND FADED, LIKE A DWARF AMONG TALL TREES. I CLIMBED THE SCABROUS IRON STAIRCASE TO THE SECOND FLOOR. I WAS THERE TO MEET A CLIENT; I WAS LATE. I MOVED PAST DARK, DUSTY WINDOWS; WINDOWS LINED WITH FORGOTTEN FRUIT. FRUIT THAT ROTTED BEFORE IT RIPENED; VICTIM OF THE LACK OF LIGHT LIKE THE HUMAN ANTHROPOIDS THAT SHARED THEIR SPACE. *AND THEN I SAW HER. SHE STOOD IN THE SHADOWS, BUT EVEN IN THE SHADOWS SHE WAS SOMEHOW BOTH LIGHTER AND DARKER THAN HER SURROUNDINGS.* THE NEON LIGHTS ON THE BOULEVARD BELOW FLICKERED AND DIED AS I REACHED OUT TO HER.

.......*BEFORE YOU LEAP*

I cheated on my man/
with Charlie Chan/
Oh Baby you're just/
got to understand/
I'm just a mystery Fan/
I'm just a mystery Fan/

Sexual Preference

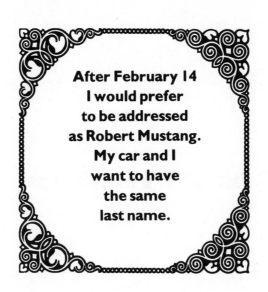

After February 14
I would prefer
to be addressed
as Robert Mustang.
My car and I
want to have
the same
last name.

_____ and I are no longer living together.
fill in blank

Our parting has been <u>Amicable/Full of hard feelings</u>.
cross one out

We <u>Do/Don't</u> want to discuss the breakup <u>Endlessly/Never</u>.
cross one out   cross one out

Thank you for your consideration.

To Whom it may concern,
I will be coming out officially
on Saturday October 12.
Everything that happens
before then doesn't count.

HOW TO MEET MEN

Many women write to me and ask, "Nicole, how can I meet men?" Most of these poor women are looking in the wrong place. I ask them to remember the words of Willie Sutton. When asked why he robbed banks, he replied, "Because that's where the money is." My advice to women who want to meet men is: *Go Where the Men are!*

From the "politics make strange bedfellows" department: According to a 1979 *Chicago Tribune* report, COYOTE is undertaking a new kind of ERA research in unratified states. Members of the California-based prostitute organization say they will kiss and tell on anti-ERA legislators with interesting or unusual proclivities.

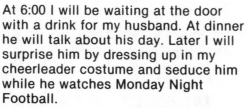

At 6:00 I will be waiting at the door with a drink for my husband. At dinner he will talk about his day. Later I will surprise him by dressing up in my cheerleader costume and seduce him while he watches Monday Night Football.

My wife will be waiting at the door with a martini. At dinner I will relate the trivial details of the day. Before she changes into her cheerleader costume I will tell her that I am in love with my dental hygienist.

Playing Doctor

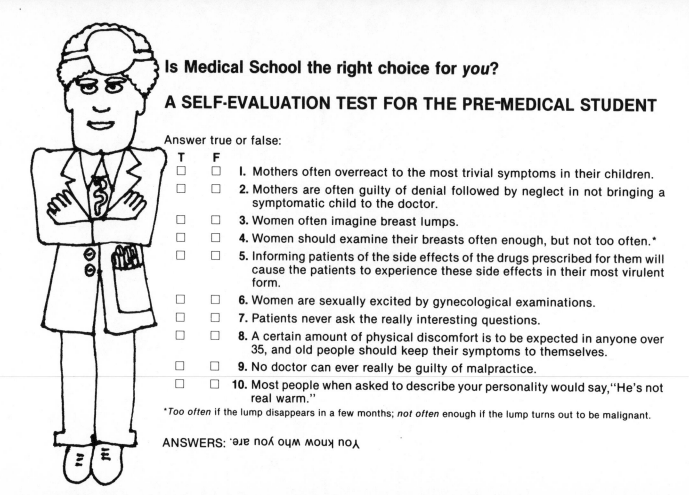

Is Medical School the right choice for *you*?

A SELF-EVALUATION TEST FOR THE PRE-MEDICAL STUDENT

Answer true or false:

T	F	
☐	☐	**I.** Mothers often overreact to the most trivial symptoms in their children.
☐	☐	**2.** Mothers are often guilty of denial followed by neglect in not bringing a symptomatic child to the doctor.
☐	☐	**3.** Women often imagine breast lumps.
☐	☐	**4.** Women should examine their breasts often enough, but not too often.*
☐	☐	**5.** Informing patients of the side effects of the drugs prescribed for them will cause the patients to experience these side effects in their most virulent form.
☐	☐	**6.** Women are sexually excited by gynecological examinations.
☐	☐	**7.** Patients never ask the really interesting questions.
☐	☐	**8.** A certain amount of physical discomfort is to be expected in anyone over 35, and old people should keep their symptoms to themselves.
☐	☐	**9.** No doctor can ever really be guilty of malpractice.
☐	☐	**10.** Most people when asked to describe your personality would say,"He's not real warm."

Too often if the lump disappears in a few months; *not often* enough if the lump turns out to be malignant.

ANSWERS: You know who you are.

I HAVE NO NEED FOR A DOCTOR. WHEN I'M OUTSIDE, I WEAR THIS MASON JAR SUSPENDED FROM MY NECK. IN IT I KEEP 3 AUREOMYCIN CAPSULES, 2 VALIUM, AND A SMALL AMOUNT OF POWDERED ELK HORN. WHEN I'M INSIDE I SIMPLY STAY OUT OF DRAFTS.

...PERHAPS YOU ARE CONVINCED THAT I SELECTED MY RECEPTIONIST FOR HER RUDENESS AND INSENSITIVITY.

OR THAT EVEN THOUGH I PAY HANDSOMELY FOR YOUR SERVICES, YOU'RE DOING ME A FAVOR.

YES, THERE'S THAT TOO.

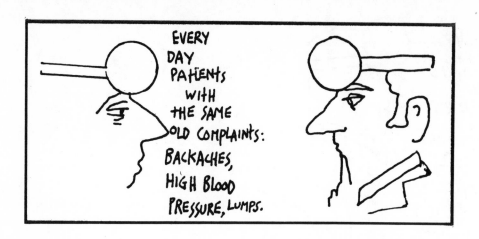

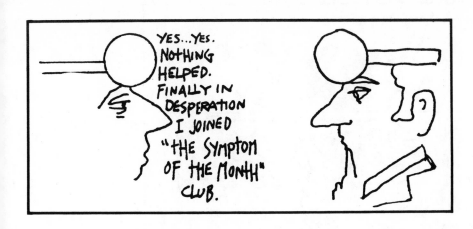

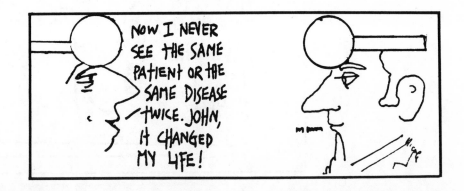

A difference of opinion

WHAT'S YOUR OPINION/ How many cats is too many?

ANYONE WITH MORE THAN FOUR CATS, HAS SERIOUS EMOTIONAL PROBLEMS.

WHAT'S YOUR OPINION/ Do you think it's fair to keep pets in a city apartment?

WHAT'S YOUR OPINION/ What would be an appropriate epitaph for your tombstone?

"She did what she could, but it wasn't enough."

"She didn't grow old gracefully."

"Irritable in death as in life."

WHAT'S YOUR OPINION/

If you could make two of your fantasies come true, what two would you pick?

I would very much like to cure world hunger and watch two women making it.

Me too.

I'd like to walk down this street just once without having some goof come at me with a microphone.

WHAT'S YOUR OPINION/

Can a woman successfully combine career and family?

Both Bob and I feel that a woman who has a career can do so only at the expense of her husband and children.

Bob is helping me to fully understand this, emotionally as well as intellectually, by dropping his clothes in little piles around the house, and by telling everyone that my children have dry skin because I neglect them.

I think, if women don't like the way
we run things here, they can go
back where they came from. That's
what I think.

WHAT'S YOUR OPINION/ Do you worry about energy?

Hey! No problem. Usually my girl friend and I go to roller disco and then boogie the night away and then directly to work. Never feel a thing.

My husband and I try to set aside a little time each night to worry about the energy crisis, usually after Yoga and before inflation.

Certainly I worry and as a scientist I feel a special responsibility to come up with a solution that will decrease our dependency on foreign oil. To that end I've been working on an energy potion. You drink the potion on October 15 and around November 15 you start developing fur all over your body and then around May 1 you start shedding and like that.

WHAT'S YOUR OPINION/ How do you plan to provide financial security in your old age?

I have a rather extensive string collection. I'm planning to sell a bit at a time. Should bring a pretty penny.

WHAT'S YOUR OPINION/ How do you feel about equality for women?

I feel that women should get equal pay for equal work.

I think it's only simple justice that women get equal pay for equal work.

Equality for women means that our potential for physical, intellectual and emotional growth be supported and nurtured. It means women recognized as full and valuable members of this society. It means being given a chance to risk, to grow, to make a contribution to a better world side by side with men.

I think if a woman's doing the same job a man is doing, she should get the same pay.

Reading by the light of the Cathode Ray

...I SPENT THOSE WEEKENDS COOKING. I PREPARED AND FROZE 500 TUNA CASSEROLES, THEN I CROCHETED A NEW ROOF FOR THE GARAGE.

...I SPENT THOSE SAME WEEKENDS GIVING THE WORD "ADULTERY" NEW MEANING

How to Meet Men:
5 Steps to Success

1. Buy an unusual dog and walk it day and night. (Little dogs with high voices are not attractive.)

2. Participate in sports that men like: pool, cock fighting, the options exchange.

3. Keep up with current events. Read the obituary notices. Haunt cemeteries, and look for bereaved men. (They're the ones with their sweaters on inside out.)

4. Visit federal prisons.

5. Stage a minor accident with a Mercedes 450 SLC or a Jaguar XKE.

RAINY DAY PICNICS

It's June! Time for elegant, lazy lunches tête à tête for deux in the park —a gaily checked tablecloth spread on the grass, the oh-so-sexy sound of bees hopping from flower to flower, some marvelous paté from that adorable charcuterie down the street, a loaf of bread, a bottle of French wine and that wonderful summer man in your life, but alors! it rains—what to do?

What fun! Take your picnic indoors. Spread a tablecloth on your living room floor, tune your radio to a country and western station—and don't forget the really super thing about an indoor picnic . . .

It gives the roaches something to do.

SUMMER BEAUTY TIPS

It's the avocado season! Time to get out your Cuisinart and whip up some of those marvelous beauty mask recipes you've been dying to try all winter.

HOW COULD I HAVE KNOWN THAT GOING TO MAVIS'S PARTY THAT NIGHT WOULD SET IN MOTION A MYSTERY, A CHAIN OF EVENTS, SO HORRIBLE, SO CONVOLUTED AND SO TEDIOUS THAT EVEN NOW MY HAND TREMBLES AS I TRY TO PUT PEN TO PAPER, AND I SEE AGAIN THAT QUEER ELFIN GRIN THAT NEVER FAILED TO FASCINATE AND AT THE SAME TIME SET MY TEETH ON EDGE . . . MAVIS. MY GOD, IT WOULD HAVE BEEN SO EASY THAT FOGGY SUNDAY TO LET THE PHONE GO ON RINGING, THAT PHONE, THAT HARBINGER OF LOST HOPES AND . . .

Shattered Illusions

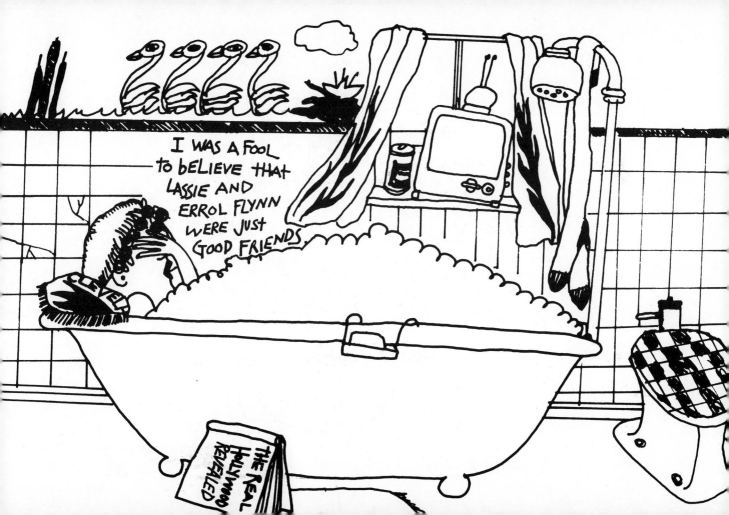

IF TRIGGER WASN'T A NATURAL BLONDE, AND SHIRLEY TEMPLE AUGMENTED HER CURLS, THEN MY WHOLE CHILDHOOD WAS BASED ON LIES.

**Commemorative Stamp
Ella Sue Whitney
First Woman to Smoke Dope on the Moon.**

When asked if she felt the women's movement had anything to do with being honored with a commemorative stamp, Ms. Whitney replied: "Certainly not, I had the qualifications and I worked like hell for the distinction."

I FEAR LUMBER YARDS.

Glamorous Secretarial Job #2

Nineteenth century career women were told that their wombs would atrophy. Now, the media warns us that women who move into executive jobs are facing increased risk of stress-related "male" illnesses like heart attacks, high blood pressure and gastric ulcers. Data for this new theory are virtually nonexistent, however, and there is in fact little agreement on what kinds of *male* workers are subject to the most stress. Writing on the subject in a May 1979 *Ms.* Magazine article, Barbara Ehrenreich concludes that it is too early to determine which women experience the most dangerous levels of occupational stress. Ehrenreich says she'd "lay odds" though on "black women, in low-paying clerical or service jobs, with pre-school children."

Knotty problems/Elegant Solutions

WOMEN WHO ARE
CONTEMPLATING
ABORTION HAVE A
NASTY RED AURA.

MY PEOPLE
REMOVE THESE
WOMEN to A
RETRAINING
CENTER SOME-
WHERE IN
FLORIDA.

HOMOSEXUALS
ALSO HAVE
AN AURA.

Some closing remarks from Sylvia